Table of Contents

3   Introduction
4   Life on Earth
7   Keys To Identification
8   Ecdysozoa (Creatures with legs)
9   Arthropoda (Creatures with jointed legs)
10   Hexapods, Diplurans and Insects
12   Pterygota picture page
14   Ephemeroptera (Mayflies)
16   Odonata (Dragonflies and Damselflies)
18   Psocodea (Lice, Barklice and Booklice)
20   Thysanoptera (Thrips)
22   Hemiptera (True Bugs)
24   Megaloptera (Alderflies, Dobsonflies, Fishflies)
26   Raphidioptera (Snakeflies)
28   Neuroptera (Lacewings and Antlions)
30   Coleoptera (Beetles)
32   Diptera (Flies)
34   Mecoptera (Scorpionflies, Hangingflies)
36   Siphonaptera (Fleas)
38   Trichoptera (Caddisflies)
40   Lepidoptera (Butterflies and Moths)
42   Hymenoptera (Wasps, Ants, Bees and Sawflies)
43   Strepsiptera (Twisted-wing parasites)
44   Plecoptera (Stoneflies)
46   Embioptera (Web-spinners)
48   Phasmatoptera (Stick Insects, Walking Leaves)
50   Orthoptera (Grasshoppers and Crickets)
52   Dictyoptera (Cockroaches, Termites, Mantises)
54   Dermaptera (Earwigs)

56   Isopoda (Woodlice, Pill Bugs and similar)
58   Myriapods (Centipedes and Millipedes)
59   Arachnids (Eight legged animals)
60   Aranae (Spiders)
62   Acari (Mites and Ticks)
64   Opiliones (Harvestmen)
66   Scorpiones (Scorpions)
68   Pseudoscorpiones (False Scorpions)
70   Solifugae (Solifuges)
72   Lophotrochozoa (Creatures without legs)
73   Annelida (Segmented Worms)
74   Mollusca (Snails, Slugs and Semi-slugs)
75   Juveniles
77   Terrestrial Larvae
78   Aquatic Larvae
79   Where Do We Go From Here?
80   Alphabetical Index

Introduction

Beetles and butterflies; spiders and scorpions; woodlice and worms. How do you tell them all apart? To say nothing of crane flies, dragonflies, bee flies and yet more butterflies. Are they all flies? If not, why call them so? If you're fascinated but confused by the beautiful world of the very small then this is the book for you.

I am a consulting naturalist living on the island of Crete in the Mediterranean sea (lucky me) and most of the photographs in this book have been taken, in the wild, by myself. Those marked ZMS I photographed whilst perusing the admirable collection at the Musee Zoologique, Strasbourg. The very few that I have not been able to photograph have been illustrated by Liz Black Dowding (www.lizblackdowding.com). You'll be pleased to know that although individual species may differ around the world their basic groupings are the same across the planet. So, wherever you live, you'll be able to use this book as a big first step to identification.

Life on Earth

For a start we had better say what we mean by creepy-crawlies. The English Oxford Living Dictionary defines a creepy-crawly as "A spider, worm, or other small flightless creature, especially when considered unpleasant or frightening." I shall expand the dictionary definition somewhat by removing the word 'flightless' as many of the little critters that you see wandering about can fly, at least at some point in their lives.

Identifying a creepy-crawly (or any other living thing for that matter) is a bit like trying to find someone's address in a strange city. The first thing you need is a map. Welcome to the City of Life.

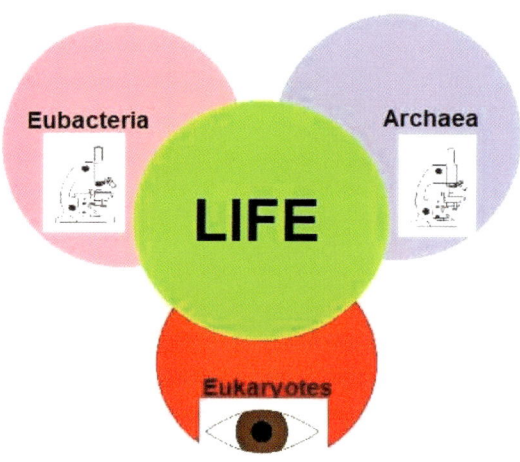

Fig. 1 The City of Life

There are three districts in the city, two of which – Eubacteria and Archaea – can only be seen under a microscope. As we can see our creepy-crawlies with the naked eye we want to enter the third district, the Eukaryotes. The Eukaryotes district contains all the macroscopic life forms that can be seen with the naked eye as well as many microscopic organisms. Biologically, the Eukaryotes are all living things that have cells containing a nucleus.

So, where do we go from here? We are looking for life forms that can be seen with the naked eye and there is one other thing that we know about them: they scurry about under their own steam quite a lot. Within the district of Eukaryotes there are four Kingdoms:

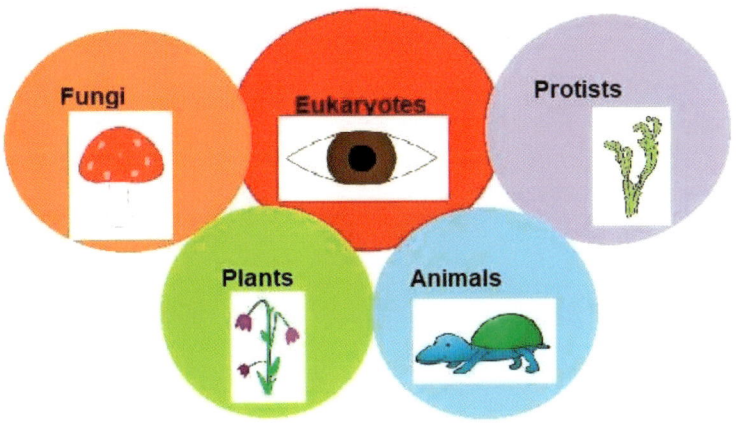

Fig. 2 Kingdoms of the Eukaryotes

Pretty simple so far, the only life forms that scurry about under their own steam are in the animal kingdom so that's the direction in which we're heading. More specifically we are looking for terrestrial creatures, those that live on land (including rivers and ponds) as opposed to marine creatures that live their lives entirely in the sea.

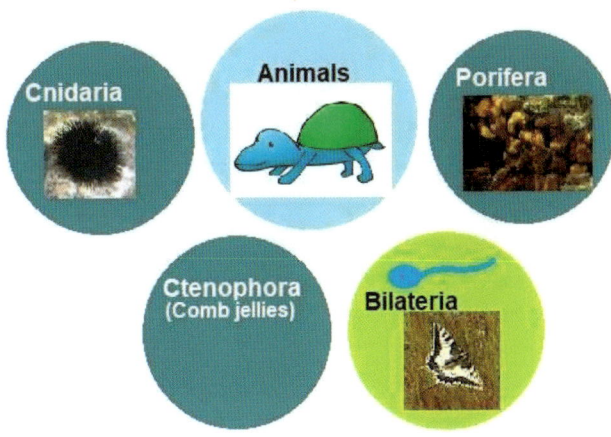

Fig. 3 The Animal Kingdom

No problems here; there is only one group of animals that are visible to the naked eye and live on land, the Bilateria. The others are all marine creatures. The name Bilateria, incidentally, comes from the fact that they have bilateral symmetry, the left side matches the right side. The only thing is, it's a description that applies to everything from butterflies to bison and honeybees to humans. Let's have a closer look at the Bilateria and see if we can't narrow it down a bit.

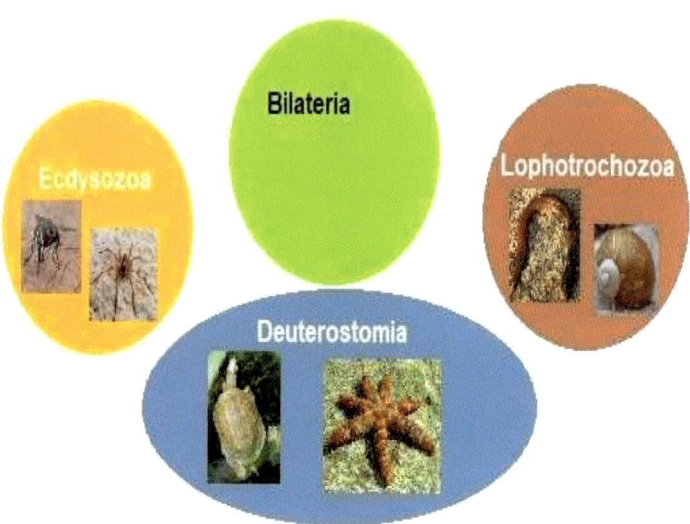

Fig 4 The Bilaterans

We are now getting to the heart of creepy-crawly territory. It looks as though we can by-pass the Deuterostomia area as it contains mainly sea creatures but also all the animals with backbones which are too big to be classified as creepy-crawlies. The Ecdysozoa and the Lophotrochozoa, on the other hand, both contain the sort of creatures we are looking for. In order to identify any one particular creepy-crawly we're going to have to put the map away and adopt a new tactic. A bunch of keys may come in handy.

The Keys To Identification

Now we get to the heart of the matter. You have a creepy-crawly in front of you (or leastways a photograph of it) and you want to know what it is. You'd probably also like to know if it's going to bite you or sting you and whether you're likely to die as a result. Will it munch its way through your vegetable patch or is it one of the good guys that keep the pests at bay?

From the last chapter we know that there are two animal groups that contain creepy-crawlies; the Ecdysozoa and the Lophotrochozoa. If you are reading this with a creepy-crawly in a matchbox on your desk or a photo on your mobile phone then now is the time to get it out.

The first thing to do is to decide which of the two camps it belongs to.

	Ecdysozoa	Lophotrochozoa
Technical description	The clue here is in the name; Ecdysis is the process of shedding the skin.	Here, the grouping together is based upon their larval development in the early embryonic stages. Basically, the mouth develops before the anus.
Practical tip	Look for anything *with* legs.	Look for anything *without* legs.
Examples		
	Go to Ecdysozoa [p8]	Go to Lophotrochozoa [p72]

Ecdysozoa

OK, so you have a creature with legs. Here is a quick question to take you to the next stage:

Is it a stubby little animal with a hard, segmented body and 8 stiff legs? Probably only just visible to the naked eye and likely found in moss or lichen?

No　　　　　　Go to Arthropoda [next page]

Yes　　　　　　It is a Water Bear in the phylum Tardigrada

Tardigrada
(Water Bears)

These are amazing little animals which are best seen under a hand lens or a low powered microscope. They can survive temperatures from −272°C to +151°C (albeit not for very long), they can spend ten days in the total vacuum of space unfazed by solar radiation and can live for ten years in a dehydrated state. Often found in moss and lichens.

Arthropoda

This is the phylum (a group of organisms with similar body plans) that contains the majority of our creepy-crawlies. They all have an external skeleton (they're crunchy as opposed to squishy in other words) and they all have jointed legs. So, if this describes your specimen then you are in the right place.

Here are a few examples of arthropods:

Insects	Spiders	Centipedes	Woodlice	Scorpions

The first thing to do in order to sort them out is to count the legs. Does your specimen have:

6 legs?   Go to Hexapods, Diplurans and Insects [next page]

8 legs?   Go to Arachnids [p59]

14 legs?   Go to Isopods [p56]

Too many legs to count?   Go to Myriapods [p58]

Hexapods, Diplurans and Insects

If it has six legs it has to be an insect, right? Well, almost. There are three critters that you may come across which have six legs but they're not insects. The reason that they are not insects is because, apart from having six legs all insects must have had, at some point in their evolution, two pairs of wings. And these three haven't had a wing between them – ever.

Hexapods

Two of these, Springtails and Coneheads are Hexapods (which just means six legs) and are more closely related to each other than to the third type, the Diplurans.

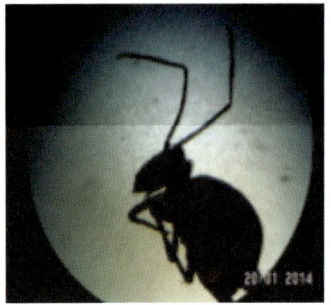

This is a **Springtail**, not sitting on a stick in front of a full moon but taken under a low powered microscope. You're most likely to come across them when you're out picking mushrooms. They're the little specks that fall out and ping across the draining board when you get your mushrooms home. That said, they are abundant worldwide and you will also come across them in leaf litter, mosses and even in the tree canopy. They are recognisable by a tail-like appendage, called the furcula, which is folded beneath the body under tension and which, when released, launch the little guys into the air like a rocket. Hence the name Springtail.

Coneheads are generally found on the floor of moist, temperate forests. Apart from the cone shaped head there are quite a few clues that make them easily recognisable. For a start, they have no wings, eyes, antennae or pigmentation. They have elongated, translucent bodies and they only walk on their back four legs as they use the front pair in place of the missing antennae, holding them up and pointing them forwards. They are so weird that you can't possibly confuse them with anything else. Like the springtails, they are very small and you need a hand lens, at least, to see them properly.

Diplurans (who's name means two tails which is a bit of a clue) are another of the small critters that you may come across when hunting through the leaf litter with a hand lens. They have no wings, eyes or pigmentation but, unlike the coneheads, they do have antennae and they are quite long. The two 'tails' (technically called cerci) come in two types: some have filamentous cerci which makes them look as if they have a pair of antennae at each end whilst others have pincer-like cerci which could make you think that you are looking at a very small earwig. Apart from the size difference, earwigs tend to be brown and black and they also have eyes.

That's those three oddballs out of the way which brings us to the majority of six legged arthropods; the **Insects**.

There are a couple of ancient, wingless insects (Apterygota) that are still with us so we'll get them out of the way first. These are **Bristletails (**Archaeognatha**) and Silverfish (**Zygentoma**).** They are not the easiest to tell apart, being small, wingless insects with three 'tails' (as opposed to the Diplurans above which have two). These 'tails' are all roughly the same length in silverfish but the middle one is usually longer than the other two in bristletails (which also tend to be a little 'hump backed' as opposed to silverfish which are flatter). Also, so I am told, if you tickle their tails and they jump then they're bristletails, whereas, if they run then they're silverfish.

| Bristletail | Silverfish |

Which brings us to the **Pterygota;** insects who either have wings at some point in their life cycle or who have had somewhere in their evolution. There are twenty seven major groups of these and just to confuse matters even more, some change their appearance very radically during their lives (think caterpillars and butterflies for instance). These I have included in the Juveniles section [p75] which is worth a quick look at some point to familiarise yourself with the available models.

Some of these groups you will be familiar with; the Odonata (Dragonflies and Damselflies) for instance and the Coleoptera (Beetles) to name but two. Others, such as the Raphidioptera (Snakeflies) may not have passed through your orbit as it were. Have a quick look at the pictures on the next page and if your specimen seems to fit the bill somewhere then check it out. If not, I'll run through all the groups, and tell you the key things to look for in each group.

Ephemeroptera (Mayflies) p14	**Odonata** (Dragonflies and Damselflies) p16	**Psocodea** (Lice, Barklice and Booklice) p18	**Thysanoptera** (Thrips) p20	**Hemiptera** (Bugs) p22
Megaloptera (Alderflies, Dobsonflies, Fishflies) p24	**Raphidioptera** (Snakeflies) p26	**Neuroptera** (Lacewings, Antlions, Owlflies etc.) p28	**Coleoptera** (Beetles) p30	**Strepsiptera** (Twisted-wing parasites) p43
Diptera (Flies) p32	**Mecoptera** (Scorpionflies, Hangingflies) p34	**Siphonaptera** (Fleas) p36	**Trichoptera** (Caddisflies) p38	**Lepidoptera** (Butterflies and Moths) p40
Hymenoptera (Wasps, Ants, Bees, Sawflies) p42	**Plecoptera** (Stoneflies) p44	**Embioptera** (Web-spinners) p46	**Phasmatoptera** (Stick Insects, Walking Leaves) p48	**Orthoptera** (Crickets, Grasshoppers) p50
Dictyoptera (Cockroaches, Termites, Mantises) p52	**Dermaptera** (Earwigs) p54			

Well, that's them. Now to sort them all out. The first thing to look for is the antennae.

Are they short and stubby? Like this or even shorter. If yes then **Diptera. [p32]**

Then, particularly if you are in the tropics, if the insect has well developed front legs right up by the head and especially if you find it in a silk tunnel then it is **Embioptera [p46]**

Next, check the mouthparts. Does it have mouthparts that resemble a hypodermic needle? If so you'll find it in **Hemiptera [p22]**

With those three groups out of the way, take a look at the wings next.

Are they easily visible and obvious? If yes, carry on. If no, go to <mark>**Apparently Wingless Beasties**</mark>.

Are they net like with veins? If yes, carry on. If no, check the antennae. If they are very long see **Trichoptera [p38]**, otherwise **Lepidoptera [p40]**.

Next, look at the tail end.
If it has two long tails and holds its wings erect: Ephemeroptera [p14]
If it has two medium length tails and holds its wings flat: Plecoptera [p44]
If it has two short tails or one that looks like a scorpion stinger: Mecoptera [p34]
If it has a snake-like head and neck: Raphidioptera [p26]
If it has no tails then **Is the head ant-like in appearance?** If yes, then **Hymenoptera [p42]** or **Psocodea [p18]**, if no
Are the wings held: outstretched or erect? Odonata [p16]; roofwise? Neuroptera [p28]; Flat? Megaloptera [p24]

<mark>**Apparently Wingless Beasties**</mark>

Did you find it living on another animal? Siphonaptera [p36] or Strepsiptera [p43]
Has it got a hard wing case that splits down the middle? Coleoptera [p30]
Does it look like a stick or a leaf? Phasmatoptera [p48]
Has it got massive back legs? Orthoptera [p50]
Is it long and thin with pincers at the rear? Dermaptera [p54]
Has it got a ten segmented abdomen? Dictyoptera [p52]
Has it got a triangular head with bulging eyes? Dictyoptera [p52]
Is it none of the above? Thysanoptera [p20]

Other than that, there are a proportion of rebel insects that refuse to obey the rules but this should help you sort out the majority of specimens that you come across.

Ephemeroptera
(Mayflies)

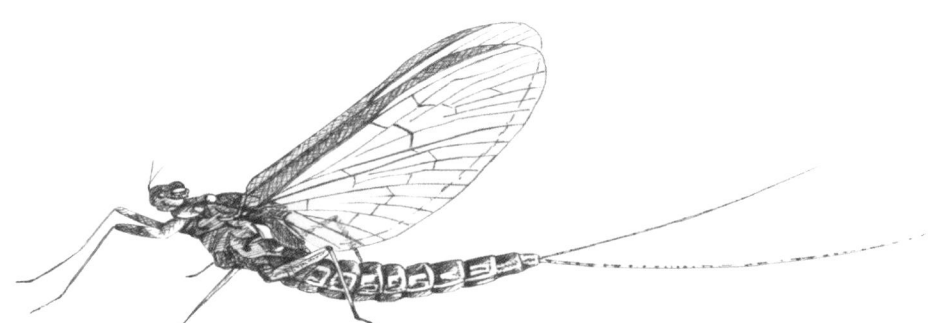

The female Mayfly lays her eggs in freshwater, either still or moving, in numbers that range from hundreds to thousands. The eggs hatch into aquatic nymphs which can live for several years in this stage before emerging in sub-adult form (unique among insects) after which they undergo one final moult before becoming fully adult. Mayflies hatch in large numbers, all at the same time, often at dawn or dusk. Their adult form is very short lived, often measured in hours, giving rise to their scientific name.

Look for: Long forelegs (used for grasping females in flight). Hindwings smaller than forewings held erect. Two long tails (cerci). Males and females similar.

Similar Groups: Plecoptera [p44] have shorter tails and hold their wings flat. Odonata [p16] have no tails.

Juveniles: Aquatic, predatory nymphs with three tails (cerci) of similar length, equal or greater than body length. Damselfly nymphs look very similar, as do dragonfly nymphs although their cerci tend to be smaller.

Do they bite or sting?

No. they are so short lived in their adult states that many do not even have mouthparts or digestive systems.

Can You Eat Them?

Yes, they are estimated to have more protein by dry weight than any other edible insect. They are eaten on the continents of Asia and Africa.

Odonata
(Dragonflies and Damselflies)

So, what's the difference between a dragonfly and a damselfly? Dragonflies tend to be more robust and bigger than damselflies and they rest with their wings out flat or forwards. Damselflies are more delicate and hold their wings together, vertically and away from their body when they are perching.

Look for: Both have long, slender bodies and large, membranous wings usually with one or two coloured cells (called pterostigma) towards the outer edge. Some damselflies however have coloured or cloudy wings and lack this feature.

Similar Groups: Neuroptera [p28] **Mecoptera** [p34] - Wing position at rest is a quick clue to differentiating between these two groups.

Juveniles: Aquatic, predatory nymphs with three tails (cerci) of similar length, short in the case of dragonfly nymphs which tend to be squatter overall and more robust than damselfly nymphs which look very similar to Mayfly nymphs.

Do they bite or sting?

They don't sting but they will give you a nip in self defence if you catch them and handle them roughly. Most don't have enough power in their mandibles to break the skin but some of the larger ones can. Incidentally, the largest living odonate is the Helicopter damselfly, *Megaloprepus coerulatus,* from Central America with a wingspan of 191mm (7.5").

Can You Eat Them?

Apparently they are a local delicacy in Bali where they are known as 'chapung'.

Psocodea
(Lice, Barklice and Booklice)

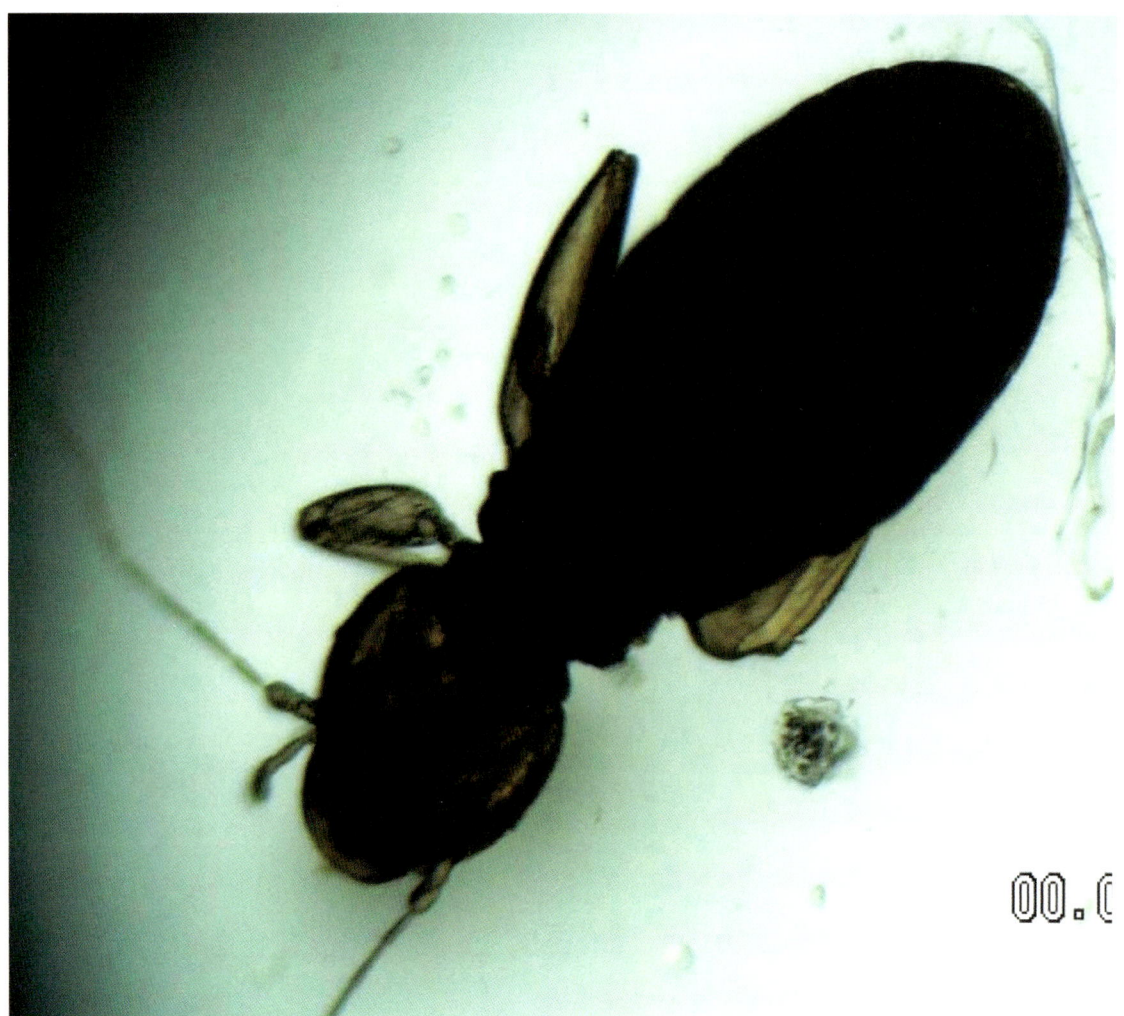

Booklice and Barklice form the order Psocoptera from which evolved the so called True Lice, the Phthiraptera. Or so we believe at the moment. Barklice are harmless creatures, feeding on lichens and algae on, or under, tree bark; booklice are nuisances, getting into stored goods and munching away and the true lice we can all do without!

Look for: The biggest clue to this group is where you find them. Booklice, as their name suggests, can be found in old books where they have a great liking for the glue on the binding. Barklice can be found on or under tree bark and the other Lice live on the bodies of warm blooded animals such as ourselves and are often specific to certain hosts or even certain parts of that host. Humans for instance host three different types of lice: head lice, body lice and pubic lice.

Similar Groups: Termites [p52] look a bit similar to the untrained eye but live in different places.

Juveniles: Smaller versions of the adults.

Do they bite or sting?

They are bloodsuckers and the human body louse, *Pediculus humanus humanus* can transmit diseases such as typhus. The head louse, *Pediculus humanus capitus*, although irritating does not transmit diseases. Pubic lice, *Pthirus pubis,* are similarly irritating but harmless.

Can You Eat Them?

Technically, yes but I can't say that I fancy the idea and they don't appear in the cuisine of any country that I know of.

Thysanoptera
(Thrips)

Although Thrips are tiny they can be a bit of a pest. They reproduce asexually which means that they can form swarms very quickly. They can infest commercially important crops and spread over 20 different viruses, all of which would appear to be a variation of the Tomato spotted wilt virus which causes brown scabs on the surface of tomatoes. As tomatoes are grown commercially in greenhouses where the thrips have no natural predators they can devastate an entire crop. They can also get into houses and infest everything from bedding to computer monitors.

Look for: Small insects (1mm or less) with linear wings having a fringe of hairs. Many thrips feed on the three Fs: Flowers, foliage and fruit where they leave tell-tale dark patches of excrement next to light areas where they have been feeding. If you can see their mouthparts you may notice that the right mandible is either vestigial or missing.

Similar Groups: None

Juveniles: Smaller versions of the adults.

Do they bite or sting?

Yes. They can cause welts, rashes and other dermal reactions but they do not transmit diseases.

Can You Eat Them?

You probably already have! As they are very small and attach themselves to commercial plants then you are bound to miss a few when you wash your fruit and vegetables unless you scrub each leaf under a hand lens. Don't worry, they're perfectly safe to eat. Just think of them as extra protein.

Hemiptera
(Bugs, Cicadas, Whiteflies, Aphids, etc.)

Cicada   **Mirid Bug**   **Scale Insect**

People often get beetles and bugs mixed up. So here is a picture of the key differences. The wing differences aren't always so obvious but the mouthparts are. The bugs are on top, the beetles below.

This is a large, diverse group of insects which, together with the Lice and Thrips, form what is known as the Hemipteroid Assemblage. The majority of hemipterans feed on plant sap but some are predatory, stabbing and sucking juices from other invertebrates. This is particularly the case with aquatic hemipteran larvae. On the whole, hemipterans are good guys. Although they suck sap out of plants they believe in sustainable harvesting and they pollinate as they travel about. Unfortunately, as well as pollen, they also tend to transfer plant viruses about too which can be a problem. Aphids and Scale insects can cause a severe nuisance to nurserymen and gardeners alike.

Look for: Sucking mouthparts sheathed within a proboscis which is capable of piercing tissues (usually plant tissues) and sucking out the liquids – typically sap.

Similar Groups: Coleoptera [p30]

Juveniles: Hemipterans do not undergo complete metamorphosis so there are no grubs to worry about. The juveniles have the same basic body plan as the adults but they have several moults as they develop and the markings and colouration often change with each moult.

Do they bite or sting?

Generally no but the Kissing Bugs of South America are bloodsuckers and can spread Chagas disease.

Can You Eat Them?

Yes, deep fried cicadas are quite a delicacy in China and parts of Africa. The Scale Insect, *Dactylopius coccus,* is the source of the red cochineal food dye and you know that lovely waxy finish that citrus fruit has in supermarkets? That's shellac (yes, the same as the wood finish) produced by lac bugs, another type of scale insect.

Megaloptera
(Alderflies, Dobsonflies, Fishflies)

From the Musee Zoologique, Strasbourg

Despite their name these are not true flies but occupy a group all on their own. The group name means 'large wings' but this is not a particularly good key to identification. These are rather elusive insects as the adults are short lived and are crepuscular or nocturnal. As the larvae are aquatic they are usually found near water and the female can lay up to 3,000 eggs on overhanging vegetation.

Look for: The hind wings fold up like a fan where they near the body. Some adult males have large mandibles which can look a bit disconcerting but they are for impressing females, not biting naturalists.

Similar Groups: Could be confused with Lacewings, Antlions [p28] or Mayflies [p14].

Juveniles: Aquatic, elongated and slightly flattened. Apart from the usual six legs at the front, many species also have a number of false legs (prolegs in scientific terminology) towards the rear.

Do they bite or sting?

Yes, they can draw blood if handled roughly but the bite is short lived and harmless.

Can You Eat Them?

Only indirectly as far as I know. Dobsonfly larvae are a popular angling bait in North America.

Raphidioptera
(Snakeflies)

These are good little predators. In the adult stage they eat aphids and mites and in the larval stage they eat the larvae and/or eggs of spiders, barklice, springtails and scale insects as well.

Look for: Extended head and thorax coupled with the lacy wings.

Similar groups: Lacewings, Antlions [p28] and Mayflies [p14] along with the Megaloptera [p24] have similar wings but none of them have that head and 'neck' except the Mantidflies which are Neuropterans [p28].

Juveniles: The larvae also show the extended head and 'neck'. They are terrestrial and often found in leaf litter.

Do they bite or sting?

No, they are totally harmless. Females have a long egg laying tube (ovipositor) which looks like a stinger but she only uses it for placing her eggs under tree bark or other secluded places.

Can You Eat Them?

Only indirectly. They make good fishing lures.

Neuroptera
(Net-winged Insects)

Lacewing

Antlion

The larvae of Neuropterans are specialised predators and are thus useful as biological control agents. If you know that your crop is being attacked by a certain entity and you can find the Neuropteran larva that particularly likes that delicacy then your problem is solved. Lacewing eggs and larvae are sold to gardeners for the control of aphids, thrips and scale insects.

Look For: Two pairs of similar sized wings held roofwise.

Similar Groups: Snakeflies [p26] and Mayflies [p14] along with the Megaloptera [p24] have similar wings but the Neuroptera don't have long necks, emerge in a swarm from water or have hindwings that fold up like a fan at the base. Mantidflies have long necks similar to the Raphidioptera [p26] but can be differentiated by their front legs.

Juveniles: These are terrestrial and many are predatory, often eating pest insects like aphids. Some camouflage themselves by wearing a coat of debris (sometimes including dead insects).

Do they bite or sting?

Yes, the larvae will have a go at you and raise a welt like a mosquito bite. If you are using them as a biological control in your garden then wear gardening gloves.

Can You Eat Them?

I don't suppose they'd do you any harm but there's not much meat on them.

Coleoptera
(Beetles)

This is the big one. About 40% of insects (and 25% of all animal life) are beetles and, from a human point of view there are good and bad beetles. The good guys include the ladybirds (or ladybugs in the US) which eat aphids, thrips and scale insects; dung beetles, without whom we'd be knee-deep and sexton beetles who are nature's undertakers. These are also useful in forensic entomology in determining the time of death. Bad guys include the Colorado Potato Beetle, Bark Beetles which were responsible for the spread of Dutch Elm Disease, and many of the weevils such as the Boll Weevil.

They can also teach us a thing or two. The mechanism that Bombardier Beetles use to project a defensive spray may soon replace the harmful aerosol sprays upon which we seem to have become dependent. They all share one distinguishing feature – their forewings have hardened to provide their hind wings with a protective casing. These wing cases are called elytra.

Look for: Hard wing cases.

Similar groups: True bugs can sometimes be confused with beetles. Check back to Hemiptera [p22] for pictures of the two main differences.

Juveniles: These come in a variety of shapes and sizes but are generally hard-headed (made of the same stuff as their adult wing cases). They do not have soft, stumpy, unjointed prolegs.

Do they bite or sting?

Yes, beetles have powerful jaws which they are quite happy to demonstrate if you handle them roughly but beetle bites are not life threatening. Blister Beetles inject a substance called cantharadin that can cause a painful blister for up to a week.

Can You Eat Them?

Yes. Beetle larvae are one of the most widely eaten insects. Darkling Beetle larvae, known as mealworms being the most popular of over three hundred species eaten world wide.

Diptera
(Flies)

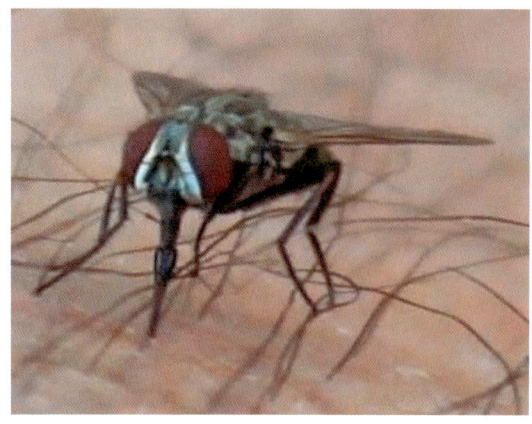

Stable Fly

Crane Flies

Drone Fly

This, I find, is the most difficult group to identify. Not only are there countless species of very diverse appearance but many of them do a superb job of mimicking bees and wasps (such as the drone fly – pictured left). "What is the point of flies?" is a question which comes up with great regularity. The answer is "to make more flies". Like every animal on Earth, including us, the meaning of life is to propagate the species and ensure its survival. What is really being asked is "what benefit are flies to us?" Given as read that flies don't have to justify their existence to us any more than we do to them, life wouldn't be so good without them. After the Hymenopterans, notably the bees and wasps, they are the next biggest pollinators on the planet. Their larvae (maggots) are used medicinally to clean wounds and remove dead tissue and where would anglers be without them? They are also a major food source for birds and other animals. On the negative side they are vectors for some serious diseases. Mosquitoes and malaria is an obvious example and house flies spread food borne diseases but, on the whole, flies do more good than harm.

Look for: The name, Diptera, comes from the Greek *di + ptera* meaning two wings. They are the only insects which possess a single pair of wings, the other pair having evolved into a pair of gyroscope-like appendages called halteres. This is how flies can turn 90 degrees at high speed and seem to disappear into thin air. In practice, however, it can be very difficult when their wings are folded over their back to determine how many pairs of wings you are looking at. The other big clue is the antennae, they are very short compared with bees and wasps.

Similar Groups: Hymenoptera [p42]

Juveniles: They have no jointed legs but some species have soft, stubby, unjointed prolegs.

Do they bite or sting?

The common house fly, along with the majority of flies, neither bites nor stings. Horse flies, deer flies and sand flies can inflict quite painful bites as they cut into the skin with a pair of scissor like appendages and then suck up the blood. Mosquitoes and certain (but not all) midges, we all know about.

Can You Eat Them?

Yes, maggots raw or fried, so long as you don't get them from a contaminated meat source. They can be extremely important if your only food source (either by choice or necessity) is lean meat. An unbalanced diet such as this can lead to a condition known as 'rabbit starvation' where the lack of balancing fats and carbohydrates causes the digestive system to stop functioning. Maggots convert the protein to fat and help to restore the balance.

Mecoptera
(Scorpionflies, Hangingflies)

From the Musee Zoologique, Strasbourg

Despite their names these are not flies and Scorpionflies are not venomous like their namesakes (they don't bite or sting). Flies have only one pair of wings; these, have two pairs. Scorpionflies are one of the mainstays of forensic entomology. Due to their predilection for human corpses they are the first to arrive and stay for about a day and a half. The presence of Scorpionflies on a victim indicates that the murder was committed within the previous 36 hours.

Look for: Long, thin wings extending beyond the body. Long snouts (rostrum). Male Scorpionflies have enlarged genitals that they hold curled above their backs like a scorpion's stinger. Hangingflies look superficially like Crane Flies, which are part of the Diptera group, until you notice the extra pair of wings.

Juveniles: Very much like small caterpillars, having jointed legs as well as stubby, unjointed prolegs.

Similar groups: Diptera [p32] Odonata [p16]

Do they bite or sting?

No (unless you are dead in which case that's the least of your worries). Despite the sinister looking tail of the scorpionfly this is used solely for reproduction purposes and is harmless.

Can You Eat Them?

Probably best not to, you don't know where they've been.

Siphonaptera
(Fleas)

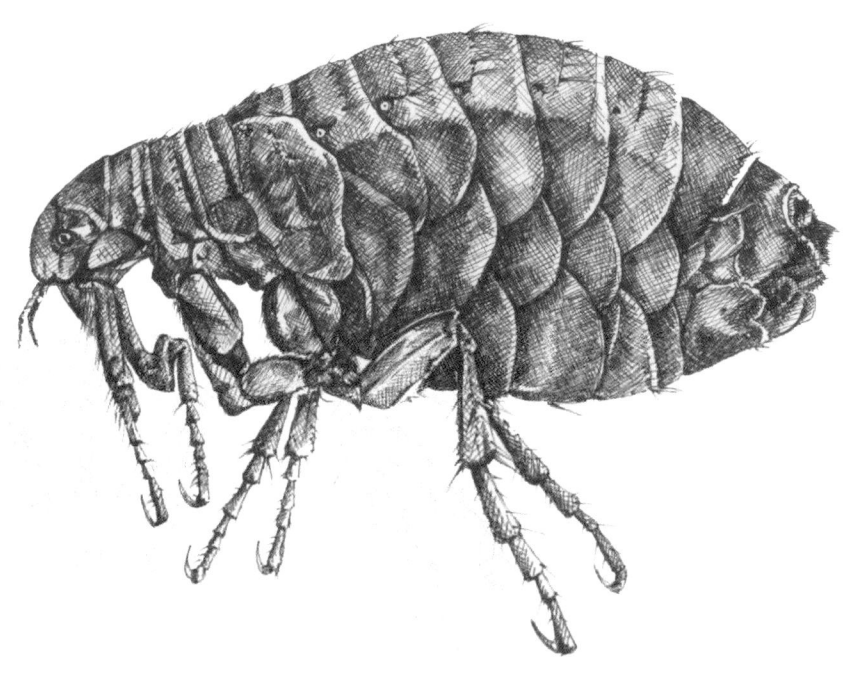

Nasty little blood sucking insects which cause many problems for their hosts. Modern fleas are wingless but are still insects as their ancestors were not. About 94% of flea species have mammalian hosts and about 3% are bird parasites. They can leap up to 15cm (about 6") and as they live on blood they are great at transmitting diseases. The Black Death in Europe (1340-1400) was a bubonic plague caused by Oriental Rat Fleas, *Xenopsylla cheopsis,* which were infected with the bacterium *Yersinia pestis.* The fleas travelled to Europe with their hosts the Black Rat, *Rattus rattus.* When the rats died the fleas jumped to the nearest available alternative host which was, more often than not, human.

Look for: Their hosts. The majority of fleas are host specific.

Similar groups: Because they both live on other animals fleas can sometimes be confused with Ticks [p62]. Ticks, however, are arachnids as opposed to insects and have eight legs.

Juveniles: Maggot like; no legs, small heads and hairy.

Do they bite or sting?

They bite, or rather pierce the skin and suck blood, but they do not sting.

Can You Eat Them?

No, they feed on you. Also, their larvae feed on the eggs of tapeworms which develop in the flea's gut, so eating fleas would give you tapeworm.

Trichoptera
(Caddisflies)

Adult

Larva

There are two major groups of caddisfly which can only be told apart from a close examination of their mouthparts.

Look for: Moth-like insects with hairy membranous wings. The antennae, however, are much longer than a moth's.

Similar groups: Lepidoptera [p40]

Juveniles: There are two distinct types of larvae. Both are aquatic and one type makes itself a fixed retreat and waits for food to pass by whereas the other type wrap themselves in silk cocoons which they disguise with debris taken from their surroundings and actively hunt for food. If you put one of these case building larvae in a jar and give it some small, brightly coloured stones to use then the results can be quite kaleidoscopic.

Do they bite or sting?

No, they are totally harmless, although a swarm of them can be a bit annoying.

Can you eat them?

I can't think that they'd do you any harm but I haven't found any recipes. Fly fishermen make imitation adults which they call sedges and the larvae are also used by anglers as bait so, indirectly, yes.

Lepidoptera
Butterflies and Moths

Scientifically, there is no difference between a butterfly and a moth. We tend to think of butterflies as bright, colourful insects that fly by day and moths as dull, brown things that fly at night. There are, however, day flying, brightly coloured moths and some very dull butterflies.

Look for: The clue is in the name; *lepido* + *ptera* means 'scaly wings' (the prefix is also the root of leper and leprosy) and it is these scales that prevent you from seeing through their wings as you can with other insects.

Similar Groups: The only group that you may confuse with a moth is the closely related Trichoptera [p38] but their wings are hairy and their antennae are very long.

Lepidopterans and man have a love-hate relationship. Although most of us delight in seeing butterflies flitting about, caterpillars are not so admired, particularly by plant growers. There's no getting away from it; caterpillars eat plants and nothing else. As most butterflies lay between 200 and 600 eggs they can do an awful lot of damage to a field of crops. On the other hand, if you have a problem plant such as happened with the Prickly Pear Cactus in Australia then introducing the Pyralid Cactus Moth from Argentina effectively dealt with the problem without the use of damaging herbicides.

Juveniles: The familiar caterpillar. Having both six true legs and short, stubby prolegs. If you look carefully at the prolegs they have a structure somewhat like a crochet hook.

Do they bite or sting?

Yes. Some caterpillars, such as that of the Pine Processionary Moth, *Thaumetopoea pityocampa,* shown below have barbed, needle-like hairs that puncture your skin. They then break away from the caterpillar and a special gland injects poison into you.

Can You Eat Them?

Yes. Adults, larvae and pupae are widely eaten around the world.

Hymenoptera
(Wasps, Ants, Bees and Sawflies)

| Ant | Bee | Wasp | Sawfly |

These are the stingers, unpleasant for some, potentially lethal for others. Many have black and yellow warning colouration but by no means all of them. And just because an insect is black and yellow it doesn't mean that it is an hymenopteran, many flies disguise themselves as hymenopterans as a survival mechanism. The stinger is an adaptation of the ovipositor (egg laying tube) so only female hymenopterans sting.

	Reaction	Treatment
	Minor	• Remove stinger immediately • Wash with soap and water • Apply a cold compress
	Moderate	• As for minor plus • Elevate effected arm or leg • Apply hydrocortisone cream • Take pain relief
	Major	• Inject adreniline using an emergency epinephrine autoinjector* • Get immediate medical assistance • Perform CPR if breathing or heart stops.

* If you know that you are allergic to bee/wasp stings then you should always carry one of these and wear a bracelet informing people of your allergy.

Look for: This is difficult as the thing that distinguishes hymenopterans from other insects is the fact that their fore and hind wings are joined together by small hooks which is not the easiest thing to distinguish in the field. Given that ants are familiar to all of us, the best way I have found to differentiate hymenopterans from other insects is from the antennae which tend to be medium length, plain and often quite hefty compared with other insects.

Similar groups: Diptera [p42]

Juveniles: Ants, bees and wasps (subgroup Apocrita) have maggot-like larvae with no legs or prolegs whereas Sawflies (subgroup Symphyta) are caterpillar-like with both true legs and prolegs <u>on every segment</u> (unlike caterpillars) and they do not have crochet hook-like appendages.

Strepsiptera
(Twisted-wing parasites)

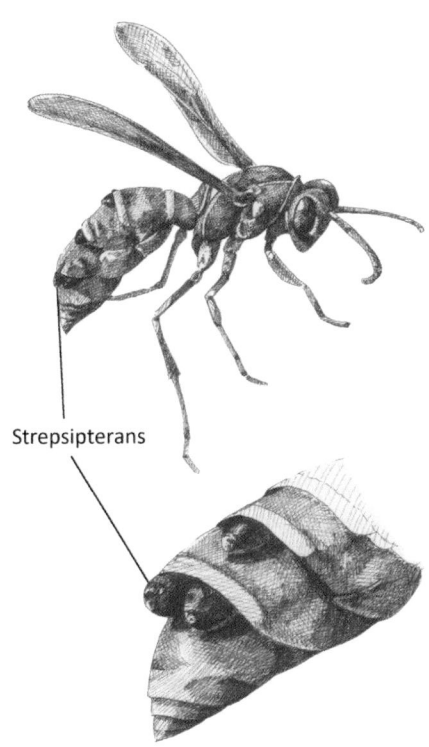

Strepsipterans

Those little bumps projecting from the wasp's abdomen is the rear end of a female Strepsipteran. In truth you are very unlikely to come across these. The males are very short lived and the females spend their lives inside their host with just the back end sticking out for mating purposes. Her young then eat their mother from the inside and then emerge briefly in order to find either a new host (in the case of the females) or the back end of a female (in the case of the males).

Plecoptera
(Stoneflies)

These are found all over the world with the exception of Antarctica and are generally to be found near rivers or streams as the eggs hatch in water and the nymphs are aquatic. They are intolerant of polluted water so the presence of Stoneflies indicates good water quality. So if you find a stonefly you know that the nearby water is clean enough to swim in. This one I found on the banks of the Derwent in Cockermouth, Cumbria, UK.

Look for: Long, segmented antennae and chewing mouthparts. The wings are long, rounded at the end, held together over the back at rest and have quite complex venation (the veins that hold the membranes in place). They also have two tails (cerci) but these may be hidden by the wings.

Similar groups: Hemiptera [p22], Trichoptera [p38]

Juveniles: These are aquatic and resemble wingless adults and so the two tails (cerci) can be easily distinguished.

Do they bite or sting?

No. They are totally harmless.

Can You Eat Them?

Yes (according to www.treehugger.com).

Embioptera
(Web-spinners)

These are primarily tropical or sub-tropical insects which get their name from the silk tunnels that they spin on rocks, trees or in leaf litter. The silk tunnels that web-spinners build are used for protection and moisture conservation. They continually extend these tunnels in search of new food sources. The wingless females do not stray far from their tunnels and winged males only emerge briefly in search of a mate.

Look for: Long, narrow, flexible bodies, 15-20mm long living in silk tunnels.

Similar groups: Coleoptera [p30] (Some Rove Beetles look similar but do not live in silk tunnels).

Juveniles: Smaller version of adults also living in silk tunnels.

Do they bite or sting?

No, they are completely harmless.

Can You Eat Them?

A bit small and fiddly. I wouldn't bother.

Phasmatoptera
(Stick Insects and Walking Leaves)

Now we come to the seriously weird. The Phasmatoptera have evolved to look like anything other than what they are and consequently are very difficult to spot unless you catch them on the move. They are mainly tropical and subtropical. Phasmids, as members of this group are called, are some of the largest insects in the world. The female stick insect, *Phobaeticus chani,* is an incredible 56.7cm long (22.3 inches) and another stick insect, *Heteropteryx dilatata,* weighs in at 65g (2.3oz.)

Look for: Leaves and sticks moving under their own steam.

Similar groups: Orthoptera [p50] Some grasshoppers look like stick insects.

Juveniles: Smaller version of adults.

Do they bite or sting?

No, but they may pinch you if you handle them roughly. Some species of stick insect, in particular, can snap their spiny back legs together around an unwary finger with enough force to draw blood.

Can You Eat Them?

Yes. The natives of Papua New Guinea spit roast any leaf insects that they find in the leaves of Sago Palms. When the legs fall off they are done.

Orthoptera
(Crickets and Grasshoppers)

So, what's the difference between a cricket, a grasshopper and a locust? The antennae: crickets have long ones and grasshoppers have short ones. Locusts are swarming grasshoppers in the family Acrididae.

Grasshoppers and crickets evoke the sound of the countryside. Like birds, each species has its own 'song'. They produce this by either rubbing their wings together or wing and leg. In both cases the wings and/or legs have small bumps on them that produce the sound which is known as stridulation.

Look for: Massive back legs.

Similar groups: Phasmatoptera [p48] Some grasshoppers look like stick insects but the enlarged back legs of the grasshopper make them easy to tell apart.

Juveniles: Smaller version of adults with underdeveloped wings.

Do they bite or sting?

They may try to bite if you handle them roughly but, as far as I know, they do not have enough force in their jaws to break the skin.

Can You Eat Them?

Definitely. There are recipes all over the Internet.

Dictyoptera
(Cockroaches, Termites, Mantises)

Cockroach

Termites

Mantis

This is a somewhat diverse group with cockroaches and termites being more closely related to each other than to the mantises. The thing that they all have in common is very short egg laying tubes (ovipositors). The cockroach is probably most people's least favourite insect (it's certainly mine) but you have to admire them. They are one of the fastest insects in the world travelling at about fifty body lengths a second which would be like you or I running at 330 kph (210 mph). Termite queens are the longest living insects in the world with some reportedly living up to fifty years. Mantises are the most common insects kept as pets.

Look for: Cockroaches and Termites: ten segmented abdomen, Mantises: triangular heads with bulging eyes.

Similar groups: Cockroaches could possibly be confused with Hemipterans [p22] and Termites with Ants [p42] but in both cases the ten segmented abdomen is distinctive. Mantises and Stick Insects [p48] look a little similar.

Juveniles: Smaller version of adults

Do they bite or sting?

Cockroaches will bite and, although they are not venomous they inhabit dirty places and thus carry a lot of harmful bacteria which can be dangerous if it gets into your bloodstream through the open wound. The best defence against cockroaches is to keep your nest clean and pour boric acid solution down your drains. Termites, in general, do not bite humans but, like ants, they have a queen, workers and soldiers that guard the colony. Soldier termites can and do bite if you attack the colony. Mantises are capable of biting but rarely do so. If you annoy them by waving your finger in front of them they are quite likely to bring their spiny front legs down and lacerate your finger which will sting like a paper cut.

Can You Eat Them?

Cockroaches: yes, if hand reared on a diet of fresh fruit and vegetables. Quite popular in Madagascar. Termites: yes, fried, steamed, boiled or raw. Mantises: Lean, clean eating machines – probably not worth the bother of collecting them.

Dermaptera
(Earwigs)

These are mainly nocturnal insects which hide away in crevices during the day. Some entomologists suggest that the name 'earwig' is related to the shape of the hindwings that vaguely resemble the shape of a human ear. Many non entomologists say that it derives from the fact that they burrow into human brains via the ear canal (an observation with no basis in fact whatsoever).

Look for: Large pincer-like cerci at the back end (the males tend to be more curved than the females).

Similar groups: None

Juveniles: Smaller version of adults.

Do they bite or sting?

Technically, an earwig can bite but they rarely do. They are more likely to give you a pinch with their cerci which can be powerful enough to draw blood. The cerci contain no venom and, though painful, a pinch from an earwig is not dangerous.

Can You Eat Them?

Yes. Quite tasty, toasted.

Isopods

Despite their name woodlice are not lice (which are insects) but crustaceans, related to shrimps, prawns, crabs and lobsters. Apart from woodlice there are some other isopods that you may come across running around the rocks down by the sea shore such as this Sea Slater.

Look for: Seven pairs of legs

Similar groups: Pill millipedes [p58] look a bit similar but they have two pairs of legs per body segment whereas woodlice only have one pair per body segment. They also have more than twice as many legs in total than woodlice.

Juveniles: Small, white versions of the adults.

Do they bite or sting?

No, they are totally harmless.

Can You Eat Them?

Yes, and would you believe, they taste like prawns. Boil up a few for a woodlouse cocktail!

Myriapods
(Centipedes, Millipedes and allies)

Centipede

Millipede

Myriapod means 10,000 legs which is a bit of an exaggeration. The leggiest millipede tops out at 750 and lives in central California. Incidentally the millipede is the earliest known terrestrial animal. Besides centipedes and millipedes there are two other groups of myriapods; the Symphyla and the Pauropoda. These are very small and live mainly in the soil.

Look for: The many legs are a giveaway. To tell the difference between the two, centipedes only have one pair of legs per body segment whereas millipedes have two pairs.

Similar groups: None (but see juveniles below).

Do they bite or sting?

Large centipedes can give you a nasty nip and, although millipedes do not bite, they produce obnoxious secretions which can blister the skin.

Can You Eat Them?

Centipedes yes, after the head and pincers have been removed. Millipedes inadvisable, due to their secretions which include hydrogen cyanide, although the Bobo people of Burkino Faso eat them (but they know how to prepare and cook them).

Juveniles: Shorter versions of the adults. The young add segments with each moult so it is possible to see a young centipede with only six legs and thus confuse it with an insect larva.

Arachnids

These are the eight legged animals. There are six major groups and we'll take each of them in turn.

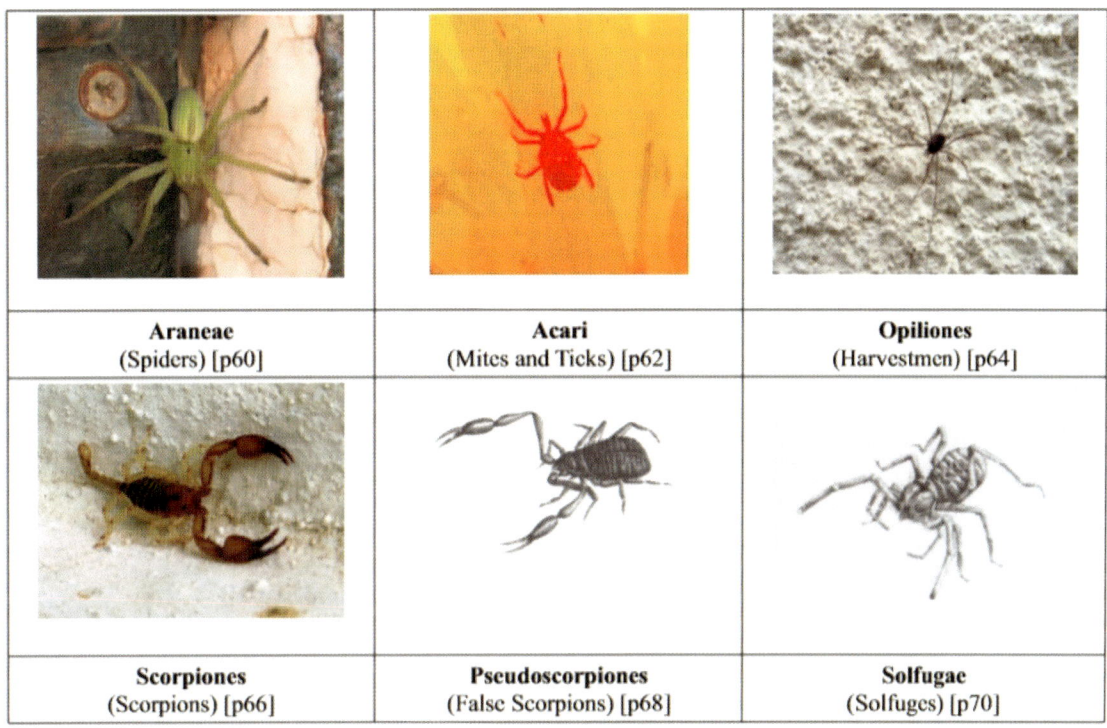

Araneae (Spiders) [p60]	Acari (Mites and Ticks) [p62]	Opiliones (Harvestmen) [p64]
Scorpiones (Scorpions) [p66]	Pseudoscorpiones (False Scorpions) [p68]	Solfugae (Solfuges) [p70]

Araneae
(Spiders)

These are probably the most feared of all the creepy-crawlies. There is no specific term for an irrational fear of spiders alone but only a term for an irrational fear of all arachnids; Arachnophobia.

Look for: Eight legs, six or eight eyes and two distinct body segments. The legs are attached to the front segment, (the cephalothorax). The rear segment (the abdomen) is not segmented.

Similar groups: Harvestmen [p64] and Solifuges [p70].

Juveniles: Smaller versions of the adults (called Spiderlings)

I always like the odd spider around the house, particularly the jumping spiders like this one; they keep the flies and small biting insects down. And, you have to admit, they are kind of cute!

Do they bite or sting?

According to Britannica there are more than 43,000 species of spider in the world, of which, less than 30 are considered to have been responsible for human deaths. Most spider bites are no worse than insect bites and clear up after 24 hours and they are all defensive bites – if you don't threaten them then they won't bite you.

Can You Eat Them?

Yes. Deep fried spiders with salt and garlic is quite a delicacy in Cambodia.

.Acari
(Mites and Ticks)

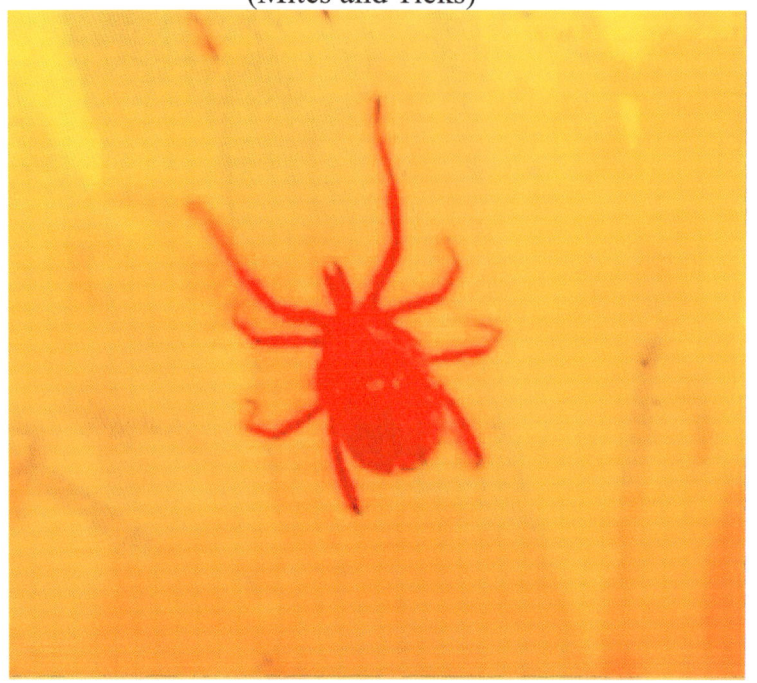

Mite

Tick

Mites and ticks are very diverse in their habits. Although the ones that we encounter most are those that affect ourselves or our pets, not all of them are parasites. Some are predatory and can be useful in controlling undesirable arthropods in agriculture, some are detrivores which help to break down forest litter and other dead organic material and some are plant feeders that can do serious damage to crops. Mites are a lot smaller than ticks and many can only be seen with a hand lens or microscope. The most familiar naked-eye mite is probably the Sidewalk Mite, *(Balaustium sp.)* pictured left. Ticks are either hairless or have very short hairs whereas mites have long hairs.

Look for: Eight legs and one distinct body segment plus a small head. The legs are attached to the main body segment. There are some worm-like mites and some parasitic mites that have fewer legs but they are very small and unlikely to be noticed on a day-to-day basis.

Similar groups: Spiders [p60]

Juveniles: Smaller versions of the adults, very often with a reduced leg count.

Do they bite or sting?

They bite and some of the Acari are vectors for nasty diseases such as scrub typhus, Q fever and Lyme disease. Mites can also stimulate an asthma attack if you happen to be a sufferer.

Can You Eat Them?

No, you wouldn't want to.

Opiliones
(Harvestmen)

These are most commonly mistaken for spiders, particularly cellar spiders, both of which are called daddy long legs in some parts of the world. This is doubly confusing as some people also refer to crane flies as daddy long legs so it is a term best dropped from your vocabulary. When you look at the body plan of a harvestman you can see that they are more closely related to mites than to spiders with their small heads and one body segment. Like lizards that can shed their tails when attacked, harvestmen can shed a leg which can twitch for up to an hour and keep a predator distracted. They cannot, however, regenerate their legs so it is a costly defence.

Look for: Eight long, spindly legs and one distinct segmented body plus a small head. The legs are attached to the main body .

Similar groups: Spiders [p60].

Juveniles: Smaller versions of the adults.

Do they bite or sting?

Harvestmen are not venomous, their fangs are too short to bite a human and they are, therefore, harmless.

Can You Eat Them?

No, one of their defence mechanisms is to produce a strong, obnoxious secretion from specialised glands rendering them unpalatable.

Scorpiones
(Scorpions)

Another little beastie with a bad (but mostly undeserved) reputation. There are some 1,750 different scorpions and only 25 are potential killers. Scorpions live all over the world except Antarctica with the northernmost naturally occurring species living near Medicine Hat in Canada 50°N. The most northerly wild (but accidentally introduced species in the 1860s) lives in Sheerness in England 51°N.

Look for: The huge claws (pedipalps) and the curved stinging tail are a dead giveaway.

Similar groups: Pseudoscorpiones [p68] but they don't have stinging tails.

Juveniles: Smaller versions of the adults usually found on the backs of their mothers.

Do they bite or sting?

Yes but the majority of scorpion stings need no more treatment than you would use for a wasp.

Can You Eat Them?

Yes. Best eaten well cooked as the cooking process breaks down the venom but they can be eaten raw if you remove the stinger and venom glands first.

Pseudoscorpiones
(False Scorpions)

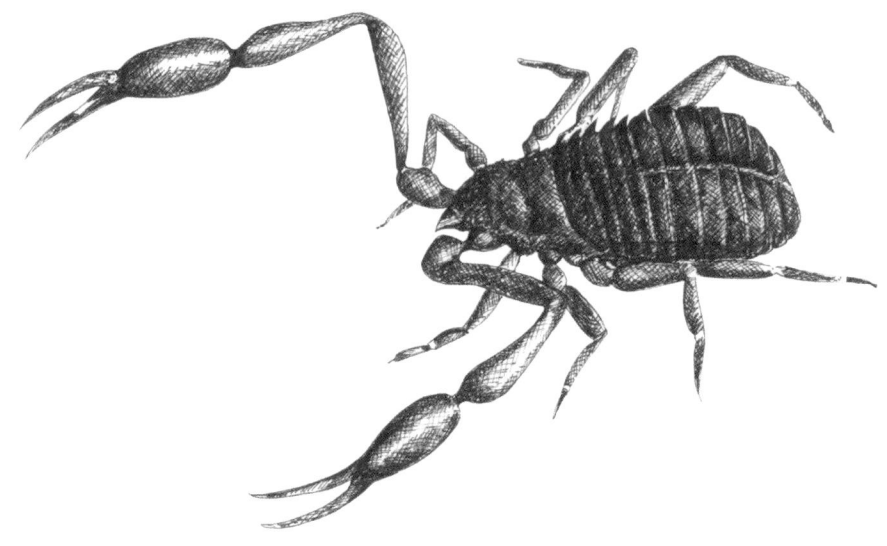

These are tiny little arachnids, usually 3mm long or less, that superficially resemble scorpions with their pincers but they have no weaponry at the back end. False scorpions are useful around the house as they eat things like clothes moth larvae, small flies, ants and mites.

Look for: Diminutive size, outsize pincers (pedipalps) and no stinger.

Similar groups: Scorpiones [p66]

Juveniles: Smaller versions of the adults usually found on the backs of their mothers.

Do they bite or sting?

No, they are totally harmless.

Can You Eat Them?

Too small to bother with.

Solifugae
(Solifuges)

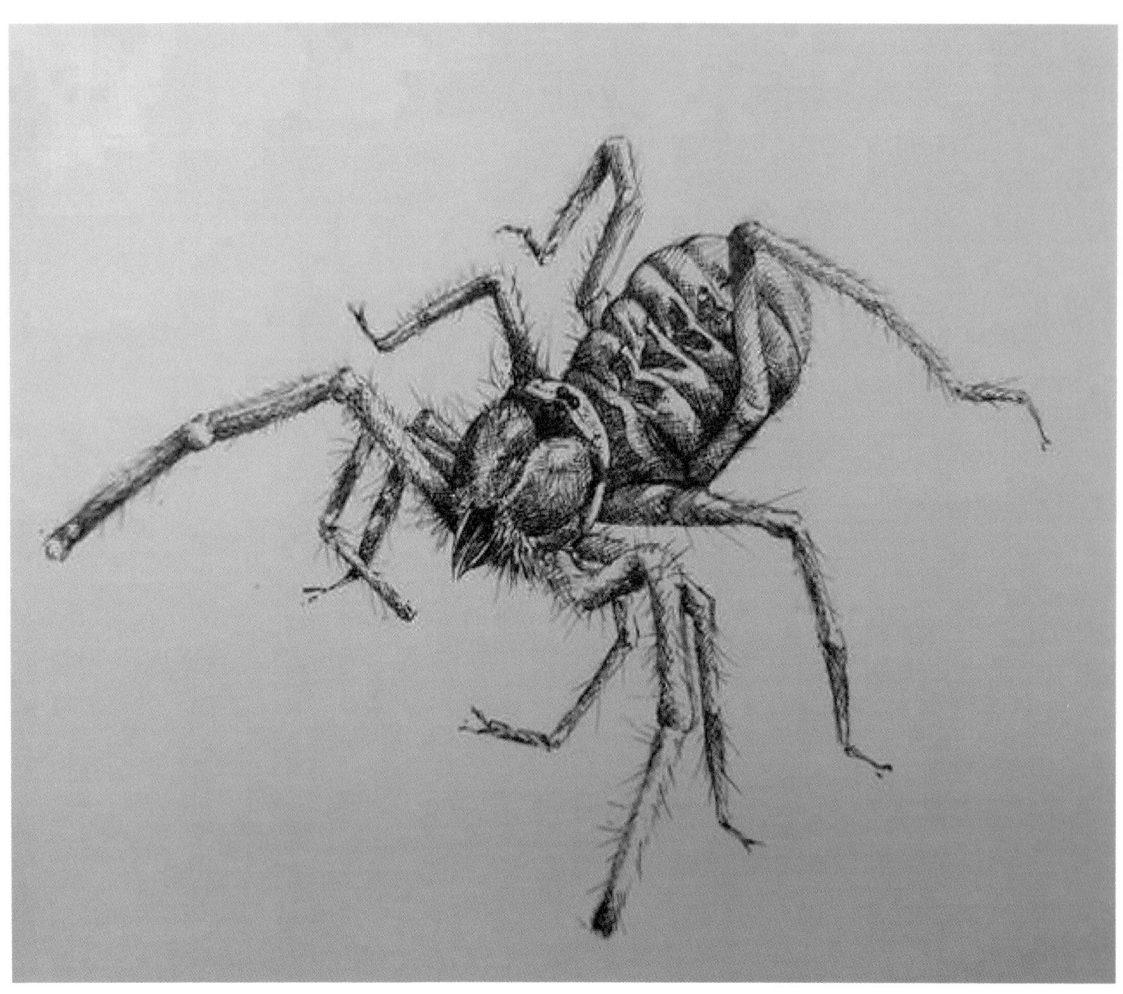

These are fairly big arachnids that live in arid and semi-arid climes and can move pretty quickly. Due to their speed and the fact that they appear quite spider-like, they engender a fight-or-flight response in us humans. Although known as Camel Spiders, Sun Spiders and Wind Scorpions in various parts of the world they are neither spiders nor scorpions.

Look for: High speed. Large chelicerae that look like an extra pair of legs at the front and two small eyes in the top of the head.

Similar groups: Spiders [p60]

Juveniles: Smaller versions of the adults.

Do they bite or sting?

They are completely harmless and have no venom in them whatsoever but they may bite in self defence.

Can You Eat Them?

I can't think of any reason why not but you have to catch them first!

Lophotrochozoa

The Lophotrochozoans are the legless creepy-crawlies, many of which are invisible to the naked eye. There are only two major terrestrial groups, the Annelids and the Molluscs. A third group, the Nemertines (Ribbon Worms) is much smaller and the terrestrial species live predominantly on islands in the southern hemisphere.

Annelids (Segmented Worms)   **Molluscs** (Slugs, Semi-slugs and Snails)

In general there is no difficulty in telling the difference between a long, thin worm; a short, fat slug; and a snail which is basically a slug with a shell on its back. If, however, you come across a short, fat worm or a long, thin slug then there is only one question to ask:

Is the body made up of ringed segments?

Yes   Go to Annelida [next page]
No   Go to Mollusca [p74]

Do they bite or sting?

No, annelids and molluscs are harmless.

Can you eat them?

Yes, worms, slugs and snails are edible and nutritious.

Annelida
(Segmented Worms)

The main annelid that you are going to encounter is the earthworm but this group also includes ragworms, which you may find on the sea shore or in river estuaries, and leeches. All of them are beneficial to us humans (although the latter may not always be appreciated).

Look for: No legs; segmented body.

Similar groups: Molluscs [p74] also have no legs but do not have segmented bodies. Millipedes [p58] have segmented bodies but they also have legs.

Juveniles: Smaller versions of the adults.

Mollusca
(Molluscs)

I won't insult your intelligence by telling you what a snail looks like and a slug is just a snail without a shell. You may not be aware however that there are also semi-slugs that fit between the two. To qualify as a snail you must be able to fully retract your body into your shell and to qualify as a slug you must have absolutely no trace of a shell whatsoever. If you have a small or vestigial shell that is too small to be useful you are a semi-slug. There are about twice as many species of semi-slug as there are slugs and about seventy times as many snails as semi-slugs. Although (and I'm guessing here), I'll bet that snails have been more widely studied and described than slugs and semi-slugs.

Look for: No legs; unsegmented body.

Similar groups: Annelids [p73] also have no legs but have segmented bodies and never have a shell.

Juveniles: Smaller versions of the adults.

Juveniles

Luckily for us over half of the creepy-crawlies just look like miniature versions of their adult form. They may have different colouration, shorter wings or other minor differences but the overall body plan is the same. However 14 of our groups undergo either complete metamorphosis – egg, larva, pupa, adult, or incomplete metamorphosis – egg, larva, adult. So here is the key to sorting out the juveniles. A word of warning; identification of larvae from a photograph is a tricky subject. As this is a *quick* guide I have simplified the keys to make the identification accurate for the majority of specimens but there will be exceptions.

Eggs

Creepy-crawly eggs come in a variety of shapes and sizes and may be laid singly or in batches on land, plants, walls or in water. It is beyond the scope of this book to describe them all. Sometimes, particularly with the lepidoptera, you can identify to species level by knowing the host plant on which the eggs have been laid. The Natural History Museum in London has an online database called HOSTS (https://www.nhm.ac.uk/our-science/data/hostplants/_) which is most helpful. The other option of course is to take some of the eggs home with you (with a good supply of the host plant where applicable) and see what they hatch into.

Shield Bug (Stink Bug) Eggs (Pentatomidae) HEMIPTERA

Larvae (which do not look like miniature adults)

I have devised a couple of tables which should help you to identify anything you find that you haven't been able to find from the adult section. Starting with one quick question:

Did you find it on land [p77] or in water [p78]?

Soldier Fly (Stratiomyidae) DIPTERA

Pupae

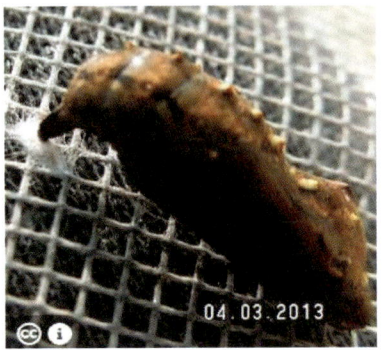

04.03.2013

14 of the groups we have looked at (all in the insect section) undergo complete metamorphosis and once they have eaten their fill in the larval state they pupate, a process in which they completely change their body plan, ready for their adult, mating state. As the insect is immobile in this stage of its development pupa cases tend to be well camouflaged, hidden away or buried to avoid predators. The groups which pupate are: Ephemeroptera, Odonata, Megaloptera, Coleoptera, Trichoptera, Plecoptera, Diptera, Raphidioptera, Neuroptera, Mecoptera, Siphonaptera, Lepidoptera and Hymenoptera.

Painted Lady (*Vanessa cardui)* LEPIDOPTERA

Terrestrial Larvae

Does it have 3 pairs of jointed legs at the front?	Does it have stubby, fleshy prolegs as well?	Are there more than 5 pairs?	Is it small and found in or on damp soil?	Does it have a long head and neck?	Does it have a hard head (like a beetle's wing case)?	Is it hairy?	Does it have an anus (a bit of black at the tail end)?	Order
Y	Y	Y	-	-	-	-	-	**Hymenoptera** (Subgroup Symphyta: Sawflies) p42
Y	Y	N	Y	-	-	-	-	**Mecoptera** p34
Y	Y	N	N	-	-	-	-	**Lepidoptera** p40
Y	N	-	-	Y	-	-	-	**Raphidiotera** p26
Y	N	-	-	N	Y	-	-	**Coleoptera** p30
Y	N	-	-	N	N	-	-	**Neuroptera** p28
N	-	-	-	-	N	Y	-	**Siphonaptera** p36
N	-	-	-	-	Y	N	-	**Coleoptera** p30
N	-	-	-	-	N	N	Y	**Diptera** p32
N	-	-	-	-	N	N	N	**Hymenoptera** (Subgroup Apocrita: Ants, Wasps & Bees) p42

Aquatic Larvae

Does it have 6 legs on the front?	Does it have leg like appendages down the side as well?	How many tails has it got?	What do the tails look like?	How does the front end (thorax) compare with the back end (abdomen)?	
Y	Y	1	Feathery	About the same	**Trichoptera** p38
Y	Y	1,2	Short &stubby	Bigger or about the same	**Megaloptera** p2
Y	N	2	Short & stubby	About the same	**Coleoptera** (Water Beetles) p30
Y	N	2	Long & thin	Bigger	**Plecoptera** p44
Y	N	2,3	Short & stubby	Bigger	**Odonata** (Dragonflies) p16
Y	N	2,3	Paddle like	Bigger	**Odonata** (Damselflies) p16
Y	N	3	Long & thin	Bigger	**Ephemeroptera** p14
N	-	-	-	-	**Diptera** p32

Where Do We Go From Here?

Hopefully you have now identified your specimen to order level. If you are still stuck you can send a photograph to my Naturalists group on facebook [https://www.facebook.com/groups/435712489794776/] and we will identify it. Mark it 'Creepy-crawly ID please' and we'll give it top priority.

If you now want to identify your specimen to family, genus or species level then there are many internet resources. I have not included links in the book as many of the sites that I use are Europe specific. The best advice that I can give is to create your own list of sites by typing the order name and your region into your favourite search engine (e.g. Lepidoptera, Europe).

Create a folder on your Bookmarks Bar marked ID Sites and store the results in there.

Steve Daniels, Crete 2019

Index

Acari   62
Alderflies   24
Annelida   73
Antlions   28
Ants   42
Aquatic Larvae   78
Arachnida   59
Aranae   60
Arthropoda   9
Barklice   18
Bees   42
Beetles   30
Booklice   42
Butterflies   40
Caddisflies   38
Centipedes   58
Cockroaches   52
Coleoptera   30
Crickets   5
Damselflies   16
Dermaptera   54
Dictyoptera   52
Diplurans   10
Diptera   32
Dobsonflies   24
Dragonflies   16
Earwigs   54
Ecdysozoa   8
Embioptera   46
Ephemeroptera   14
False Scorpions   68
Fishflies   24
Fleas   36

Flies	32
Grasshoppers	50
Hangingflies	34
Harvestmen	64
Hemiptera	22
Hexapods	10
Hymenoptera	42
Insects	10
Isopoda	56
Juveniles	75
Lacewings	28
Lepidoptera	40
Lice	18
Lophotrochozoa	72
Mantises	52
Mayflies	14
Mecoptera	34
Megaloptera	24
Millipedes	58
Mollusca	74
Moths	40
Myriapods	58
Neuroptera	28
Odonata	16
Opiliones	64
Orthoptera	50
Phasmatoptera	48
Pill Bugs	58
Plecoptera	44
Pseudoscorpiones	68
Psocodea	18
Pterygota	12
Raphidioptera	26
Sawflies	42
Scorpiones	66
Scorpionflies	34
Scorpions	66

Segmented Worms	73
Semi-slugs	74
Siphonaptera	36
Slugs	74
Snails	74
Snakeflies	26
Solifugae	70
Solifuges	70
Stick Insects	48
Stoneflies	44
Strepsiptera	43
Termites	54
Terrestrial Larvae	77
Thrips	20
Thysanaura	20
Trichoptera	38
True Bugs	22
Twisted-wing parasites	43
Walking Leaves	48
Wasps	42
Web-spinners	46
Woodlice	56

Printed in Poland
by Amazon Fulfillment
Poland Sp. z o.o., Wrocław

50937919R00049